ideals
FRIENDSHIP

FRIENDSHIP'S A NAME TO FEW CONFIN'D ⚬ THE OFFSPRING OF A NOBLE MIND ⚬ A GENEROUS ⚬ WARMTH WHICH FILLS THE BREAST ⚬ AND BETTER FELT ⚬ THAN E'ER EXPREST ⚬

ISBN 0-8249-1044-3

Publisher, Patricia A. Pingry
Editor, Ramona Richards
Art Director, David Lenz
Permissions, Kathleen Gilbert
Copy Editor, Susan Dubois
Phototypesetter, Angela Smith
　　　　　　　　　Tammy Walsh

IDEALS—Vol. 43, No. 5 August MCMLXXXVI IDEALS (ISSN 0019-137X) is published eight times a year,
February, March, May, June, August, September, November, December
by IDEALS PUBLISHING CORPORATION, Nelson Place at Elm Hill Pike, Nashville, Tenn. 37214-8000
Second class postage paid at Nashville, Tennessee, and additional mailing offices.
Copyright © MCMLXXXVI by IDEALS PUBLISHING CORPORATION.
POSTMASTER: Send address changes to Ideals, Post Office Box 148000, Nashville, Tenn. 37214-8000
All rights reserved. Title IDEALS registered U.S. Patent Office.
Published simultaneously in Canada.

SINGLE ISSUE—$3.50
ONE-YEAR SUBSCRIPTION—eight consecutive issues as published—$15.95
TWO-YEAR SUBSCRIPTION—sixteen consecutive issues as published—$27.95
Outside U.S.A., add $4.00 per subscription year for postage and handling.

Front and back covers by Fred Sieb
Inside front cover by Gerald Koser
Inside back cover by Ken Dequaine

July
in
High

The rolling year has shifted gear,
And summer's into high.
The corn and wheat enjoy the heat.
All nature loves July.

This month, part spring, has hope to bring
For growth in field and man.
This month, part fall, portends to all
God's changing changeless plan.

Margaret Rorke

Photo Opposite
SUMMER FIELD
Gottlieb Hampfler

Summer Gold

Summer, streak the heavens with your golden fingers;
Gild the filigree of the spider's silk-lace web;
Kiss the weeping willow, leaning gnarled and old,
Then spin its boughs with shimmering threads
Of lovely, lovely, summer gold.

I see you all about me, Summer, your vistas so resplendent
In the morn's first glint of lemon light,
Capturing the yellow-winged finches
In their flashing, darting, joyous flight.
And there, within her sun-jeweled, tangled nest,
The lark hides 'way her golden breast.

You gleam in the waving flags of goldenrod,
In buttercups that gently nod, and across the meadow
Daisy-kissed, colts frolic in the rainbow's pastel mist.
There's a feeling of contentment as these treasured days unfold,
And I thank you, God, for blessing us
With this lovely, lovely, summer gold.

Rose Emily Houston

Summertime

The magic that is summertime
Has come to stay awhile,
With warm, enchanted hours
And lovely, radiant smiles.

The magic that is summertime
Is spread over forest and field,
Emerald green in splendor
Before the harvest yield.

The sparkling surf and golden sands
Offer wonders to behold;
Picnics, hikes and boating
Are enjoyed as hours unfold.

Evenings filled with twinkling stars,
A yellow moon above;
The crickets singing serenades
And all the world in love.

The magic that is summertime
Is truly filled with bliss,
A time when God walks very near
Bestowing Heaven's kiss.

LaVerne P. Larson

Sonnets

Barefoot poets, aged three and four,
Write sonnets on a sandy shore;
Castles shine in splendid beauty,
Lapped by waves and filled with booty.

Tides may come and tides may go
And the sands of time run low,
But sleeping poets of three or four
Dream of castles on the shore.

Stars and starfish swim in the moat;
A seashell makes a lovely boat.
Sea horses are legionary,
The tower their sanctuary.

Keep the sonnets on the shore;
Keep the dreams forevermore.
The world needs castles on the shore;
It needs them now as never before.

Betty Hunter

Photo Opposite
ROLLING SURF
Ken Dequaine

Readers' Reflections

Friendship's Glow

There's a feeling in the heart of me
That fills me with a glow.
And I know where it's a-coming from—
It's from the folks I know.

It's the love they all hold for me,
And have been holding quite a while.
It comes to me in birthday cards,
In hugs, handshakes and smiles.

Or when they come a-calling,
Or ring me on the phone,
Just to ask how I'm a-doing
To let me know I'm not alone.

There's no feeling quite can match it.
I'm sure God sends it from above,
Just to tell me part of Heaven
Will be having friends to love.

John J. Pepping
Los Angeles, CA

A Friend Like You

I have no gold to give you
For the many things you do,
And I know you wouldn't take it
If I offered it to you.

You are always there to aid me,
You bring sunshine every day,
Always sharing—always caring,
In your kind and humble way.

May the good Lord bless and keep you,
As I'm sure he's bound to do.
I've been richly blessed and fortunate
To have a friend like you.

Bill Carr
Gladwin, MI

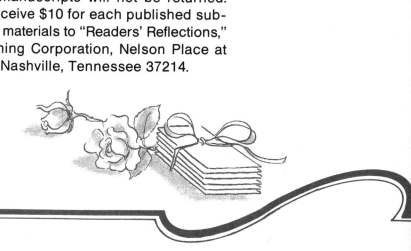

Editor's Note: Readers are invited to submit unpublished, original poetry, short anecdotes, and humorous reflections on life for possible publication in future *Ideals* issues. Please send copies only; manuscripts will not be returned. Writers will receive $10 for each published submission. Send materials to "Readers' Reflections," Ideals Publishing Corporation, Nelson Place at Elm Hill Pike, Nashville, Tennessee 37214.

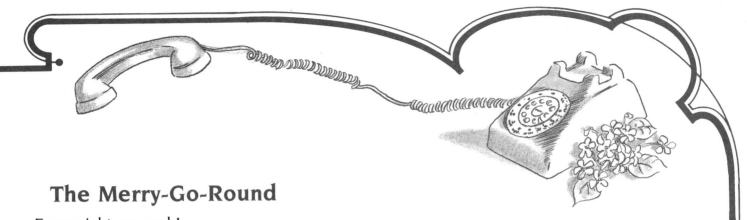

The Merry-Go-Round

Every night you and I
Would walk our tiny town.
We talked of all the dreams we had
And watched the world go round.

Our special place that no one knew
Is where we'd always go.
We'd reminisce and dream some more
Of all we had yet to know.

Those moments faded into shadows
And left nothing to be found,
But the shadows of our dreams
Still ride the merry-go-round!

Bruce Benzel
Fond du Lac, WI

Summer Joy

The smell of summer's in the air,
Green grass, blue sky—everywhere.
How can I stand such joy to my senses?
I think I'll go jump all the fences.
I'll fling wide open every door.
I'll sprout some wings so I can soar.
I'll sing each song that fills my heart.
All this rapture to others I'll impart.
Can't you feel it? Can't you see?
Earth's beauties manifest to me.
Where's someone who feels it too?
Come—I'll share it all with you!

June C. Bush
Rexburg, ID

The Value of Friendship

Imagine life without friends. How dull would be the path walked alone. How empty would be the hours with no one to fill them with laughter and a smile.

In all creation, man is the only creature endowed with the ability to laugh. Although they bring beauty to our world, flowers and trees, birds and animals cannot laugh. Only mankind was given the gift of laughter. Without friends, the gift is bare. It is the only thing given away that always returns. It is a two-way street whereupon both parties are ennobled.

Anyone can be a fair-weather friend. The value of friendship is measured after all the tears have dried. True friends are the stepping-stones which enable us to overcome the stumbling blocks of life.

It is said that "the path to salvation is narrow and as difficult to walk as a razor's edge." How comforting it is to walk it with a friend.

Imagine life without friendship? Imagine spring without flowers or a day without sunshine! It truly is one of God's greatest gifts.

Clay Harrison
Tampa, FL

I Grew Up in the Desert

I grew up in the desert hating sand
And rocks and cactus, and I always dashed
Outside when rain clouds drenched my thirsty land
And soothed what stinging springtime winds had lashed.
I'd laugh and lift my hands and face to feel
The pelting drops that cooled the summer heat;
I'd stand and watch the wild gray wetness reel
And fall upon the sunburnt sand and beat
The struggling green with water-life. I dreamed
Of forests thick with tree and leaf, of great
Green hills and mossy paths, of fields that seemed
To sway with breezy grass, but as of late
I live where rain is cheap and what I prize
Is not lush green but dry and sunny skies.

Barbara Hudson

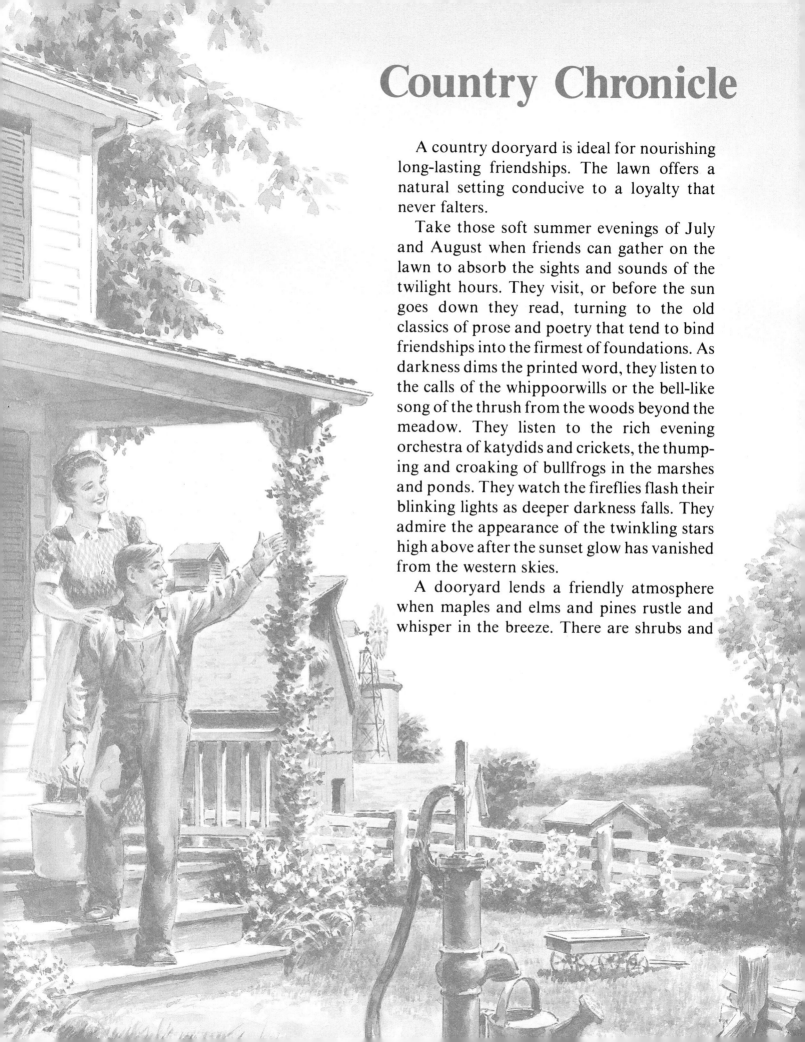

Country Chronicle

A country dooryard is ideal for nourishing long-lasting friendships. The lawn offers a natural setting conducive to a loyalty that never falters.

Take those soft summer evenings of July and August when friends can gather on the lawn to absorb the sights and sounds of the twilight hours. They visit, or before the sun goes down they read, turning to the old classics of prose and poetry that tend to bind friendships into the firmest of foundations. As darkness dims the printed word, they listen to the calls of the whippoorwills or the bell-like song of the thrush from the woods beyond the meadow. They listen to the rich evening orchestra of katydids and crickets, the thumping and croaking of bullfrogs in the marshes and ponds. They watch the fireflies flash their blinking lights as deeper darkness falls. They admire the appearance of the twinkling stars high above after the sunset glow has vanished from the western skies.

A dooryard lends a friendly atmosphere when maples and elms and pines rustle and whisper in the breeze. There are shrubs and beds of flowers and ferns brought in from the wilds to bring nature close to the door. One is never far removed from woods and thickets, from swamps and bogs, from fields and hill pastures.

There are rustic buildings nearby, the well house and garage and the now-unused smoke-house. The woodbine climbs and colors their walls of stone. There are clumps of bittersweet that will soon transform the creekside wall into a deep reddish-orange that will gleam and glow in the sun of late afternoons once autumn comes. The sumac by the fence is already assuming its bright scarlet hues.

For countless summers now a man has thought of the lawn as his parlor out-of-doors, its soft resilient carpet of grass creeping up to the stone walks around the house. It is a place that teems with inspiration and song, one that offers rest and reflection.

In such an atmosphere of peace and serenity, it is little wonder friends can dream those dreams that reveal a sense of true tranquillity that so appeals to connoisseurs of rural surroundings. They find no limit to Nature's varied talents in the field of fine arts. She is the painter, the philosopher, the author of the greatest prose and poetry, the composer and singer of the purest songs.

Lansing Christman

In an Old Garden

Here hollyhocks grew colorful and tall,
And mignonette its gentle fragrance spread
Across the brilliant, morning-gloried wall,
While elfin pansies clustered in their bed.

Baby's breath lay like a dainty mist,
Bright foxglove clung like jewels to its stalks,
Gold butterflies the pale snapdragons kissed,
Forget-me-nots outlined the garden walks.

Heartsease and dainty sprigs of feverfew
Grew in this garden of an olden time,
Pale lavender and larkspur, tall and blue,
Small Canterbury bells would softly chime.

As twilight came with shadowy, gray wing,
The sundial knew no more the passing hours,
And dew pearls to the heliotrope would cling,
Sweet lethargy crept o'er the drowsy flowers.

Old garden dreaming in the summer night,
Lit by the fireflies' small flitting spark
Or silvered by the moon upon its flight.
You still breathe fragrance in the quiet dark.

Ruth B. Field

The Secret

I watched him tend his flowers—
So gentle, thoughtful, wise.
A glowing admiration
Showed in the gardener's eyes.

He walked and talked among them
And grew to know them well.
He loved them with a passion,
And loving casts a spell.

And now I know his secret
(I should have from the start):
His flowers, like his friendships,
Are tended with the heart.

June Masters Bacher

Friendship

I let my ship sail out to sea
Across the silvery blue
Of friendship's deep and lasting ties
And steered it straight to you.
I filled its hold with pleasant thoughts
And memories by the score,
Along with golden dreams to share
And sent them to your door.

And when my little sailing ship
Will find its way to you,
I hope you'll know that it is filled
With friendship's bonds so true.
And if your thoughts are happy thoughts
And joys are full and free
Just turn the little ship around
And sail it back to me.

Carice Williams

Man's Need

Just to need to be needed by someone
Is the whole of man's mission on earth.
It's the total—the sum of his purpose.
It's the ultimate goal of his worth.

In a world that is wanting in freedom,
In a nation with pockets of poor,
In a city with problems a-plenty,
There is need for man's goal, to be sure.

There is need on the busiest homefront.
There is need where it's quiet and lone.
He who finds him a spot where he's needed
Fills the paramount need of his own.

Margaret Rorke

Anyone for a Kitten?

A black and white kitty came calling one day
And—though we resisted—elected to stay.
We had strong suspicions she thought it her right
For she was so welcomed by our tom "Midnight."

He seemed more than willing to "stake her a claim"
And made us to know that he fell for the dame.
Well, time has passed by. She has stayed by his side;
He, the happy groom, with an "alley cat" bride.

It's double of everything, milk and of meat—
(Their soft-hearted master gives many a treat!)
We noticed that lately, with spring scarce begun,
The female seems only to bask in the sun.

While Midnight goes forth on a gay hunting spree
His lady stays home, as content as can be.
This morning she stayed in her shelter indoors.
And busied herself with some motherly chores.

'Gainst any intruder, she strongly defends,
And Midnight is giving cigars to his friends.
Five furballs were born! They would fit in a mitten!
We're frantically asking, "Don't YOU want a kitten?"

Edna Moore Schultz

The Hiding Place

We have a little hiding place,
  my brother and I.
A special little hiding place out under
  the sky,
At the end of the meadow, at the bottom
  of the cliff,
We can arrive there in just a little jiff!

Just grab the old rope tied to the old
  tree,
And slide down the hill, oh so fast and
  free!
But be very careful! Watch out where
  you land!
Be sure to miss the water and hit the
  softer sand!

Now you're in our "Hiding Place."
Look around for a comfortable space.
Step over the stream, wade through the
    grass;
Lean against a tree for some time
    to pass.

This "Hiding Place" is where all our
    plans are made,
Where our time is whiled away in the
    Quiet shade.
A special place where our lifelong
    Dreams are born,
A soothing place where our broken
    Hearts are mourned.

This is the place where we conquer and
    thrive,
Our little spot on earth that makes us
    glad we're alive.
Here our childhood memories are
    forever stored,
Never-ending memories which will
    always be adored.

Loni

A Friend

A friend, beloved, tried and true,
An old one, shared, or one quite new;
There is nothing greater that even gold could buy,
Than a real, true friend under God's blue sky.

A friendship, like a chain of gold,
Is molded link by link,
In sharing smiles and tears alike,
And all the thoughts we think.

The joy of being wanted
In the friendship that we share
Gives life a tender meaning
And a love beyond compare.

It's good to feel the handclasp
Where days be gay or sad,
And know that other hearts respond
In good days or in bad.

As steadfast as warm summer days
A friend will ever be,
Binding close a friendship
That will live eternally.

Edith M. Helstern

A Boy
and His Dog

Just wandering down a winding path,
A picture of contentment and joy,
A soft and wiggly puppy
And a freckle-faced, barefoot boy.

With fishing pole on his shoulder
And his puppy by his side,
He's headed for a gurgling stream
Where all the big fish hide.

Skin so smooth and golden-tanned
From the sun of summer days,
Sifting the dust between his toes
While his puppy dashes at play.

Tattered straw hat on his head,
Whistling a merry song,
A bag of goodies tucked under his arm
And his puppy tagging along.

Golden locks of tousled hair
Blowing in his face,
Nary a care in all the world
But to beat his puppy in race!

Ruth H. Underhill

To a Cat

Cans of cat food, pounds of liver.
Sometimes it seems I am the giver
Of attention constantly,
But, of course, from you to me
There is fond attention, too,
Given to me as you grew.
In my lap or on my bed,
While I stroke your furry head,
You survey me with green eyes
In which deep affection lies.
Through the months and through the years
Plain to me this fact appears:
You have given me so much
For every meal and loving touch.

Louise Darcy

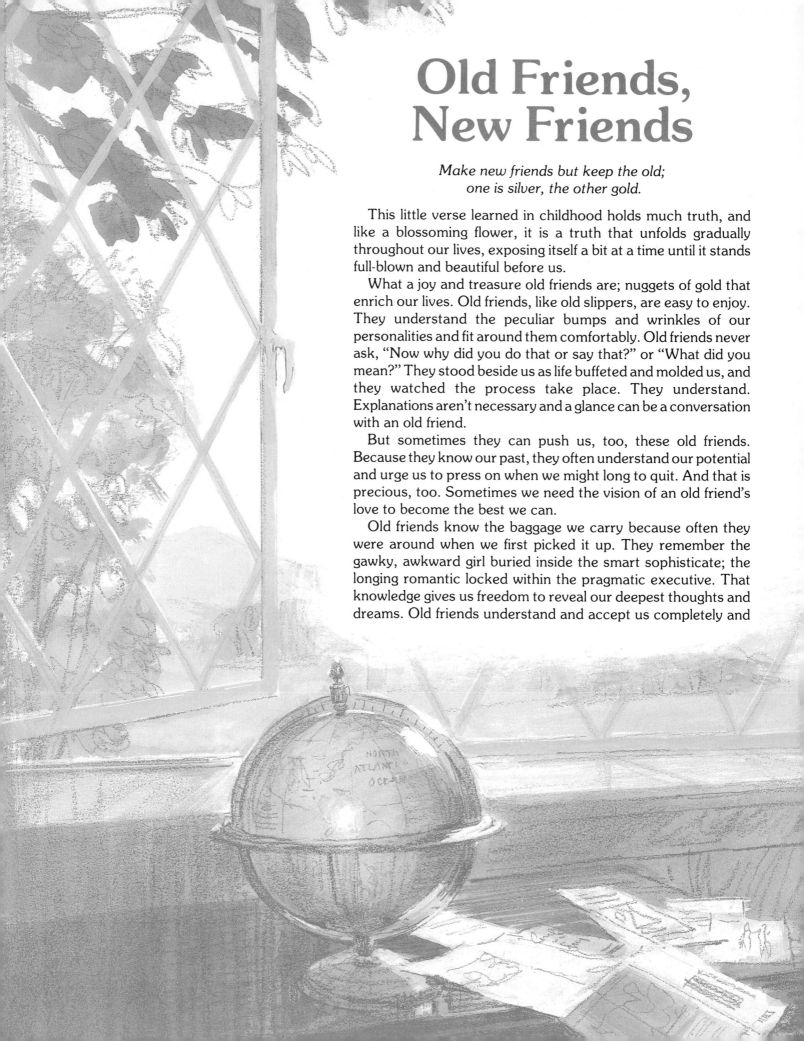

Old Friends, New Friends

Make new friends but keep the old;
one is silver, the other gold.

This little verse learned in childhood holds much truth, and like a blossoming flower, it is a truth that unfolds gradually throughout our lives, exposing itself a bit at a time until it stands full-blown and beautiful before us.

What a joy and treasure old friends are; nuggets of gold that enrich our lives. Old friends, like old slippers, are easy to enjoy. They understand the peculiar bumps and wrinkles of our personalities and fit around them comfortably. Old friends never ask, "Now why did you do that or say that?" or "What did you mean?" They stood beside us as life buffeted and molded us, and they watched the process take place. They understand. Explanations aren't necessary and a glance can be a conversation with an old friend.

But sometimes they can push us, too, these old friends. Because they know our past, they often understand our potential and urge us to press on when we might long to quit. And that is precious, too. Sometimes we need the vision of an old friend's love to become the best we can.

Old friends know the baggage we carry because often they were around when we first picked it up. They remember the gawky, awkward girl buried inside the smart sophisticate; the longing romantic locked within the pragmatic executive. That knowledge gives us freedom to reveal our deepest thoughts and dreams. Old friends understand and accept us completely and help us know that what we were does not negate what we have become.

Old friends aren't afraid to share our sorrows. Their handclasp transmits love and caring more eloquently than words or flowery expressions of grief. They know the price we paid in time and energy and emotion, and when it all falls through, they stand beside us and their support helps us maintain our balance.

Old friends are a treasure of inestimable value who give themselves to help enrich our lives. But what of new friends? They are faces whose names we've only learned; mysterious packages of personality we're just a bit afraid to open. These are treasures of a different kind; the sparkling, shining silver that brings to light new facets of ourselves.

For new friends challenge us to stretch and reach outside ourselves—and inside, too. To try new things, acquire new skills, make new bonds with people who were strangers yesterday. They shake us from complacency and dare us to find within ourselves attributes we never knew we had.

New friends know nothing of our history except what we choose to reveal. They allow us the freedom to begin again, unencumbered by past failures and mistakes. Fresh as a silver morning, new friends permit us to embark on a new day at any point in life. They never saw the troubled teen, the unsure newlywed, the frazzled young mother. They see the now, the end result of all the yesterdays and the promise of tomorrow. New friends are the future. Their shining brightness calls us to go on without regret; to do something we've never done and be someone we've never been before.

Let us, then, not hide ourselves in the golden glow of an old friend's challenges. Let us learn to meld the two, enriching our lives immeasurably as the gold and silver intertwine, linking our lives in a precious chain of friendship.

Pamela Kennedy

Her Flowers Fair

How well her flowers grow,
Nurtured by her love, her tender care,
How beautiful their blooms,
So vivid, delicate and fair!

Along the rustic fence
Her scarlet roses climb,
The highlight of the farm
With fragrances so divine.
And by the pathway to the house,
Her pansies flourish in a row,
In brightest yellow, deepest purple,
Exultant in the sunlight's glow!

In borders long and deep,
She tills mindfully with her hoe,
Upending only pesky weeds
So luxuriantly her flowers may grow.
And then she adds a strong support
To a delphinium that leans,
And removes a withered bloom
From a peace rose that she esteems.

Beside the garden wall,
Her sweet peas cleave and climb,
And bloom in delicate pastels
In Nature's own design.
And where the shasta daisies
Cast their brilliant glow,
She picks her favorite blooms,
Petalled beauties white as snow!

With straw sunhat and cotton gloves,
Small trowel and sharpened hoe,
She finds contentment in each day
Amidst her flowers while they grow.
And as she richly gives
Of her love and tender care,
She finds her love threefold returned
By their blossoms bright and fair!

Joy Belle Burgess

Photo Opposite
NEIGHBORLY GARDEN
Syd Greenberg
Cyr Color

Mary Was Her Name

Friendships are treasured rewards of life, especially for country folks. Country homes and farms are often isolated from the nearest neighbor and many miles from a town. When I was a little girl, it was delightfully exciting when one of my parents' friends was going to call on us. Amidst a flurry of activity, our house would be readied for company, and a full-course dinner would be prepared. My family, with even the kids spic and span, would gather by the door to welcome the visitor. I was impressed by the warm welcome our guest received, and learned at an early age that friends are special and friendships are to be valued.

When I was a young bride of nineteen, my husband and I settled on a farm in Pennsylvania. I was happy most of the time, but there were times when I was sad and very lonely. Everyone I knew was back in New York State; I missed my large family and all the relatives, neighbors and friends so much that I was positive that I could never be content without them close by.

"You're sure to meet new friends," my mother would soothe, as I told her how lonely it was so far from home. Mom's prediction soon came true! Before long, I became acquainted with a very friendly lady on the telephone party line who was known to everyone in Locust Hill as "Mary." There were twenty families on our party line and it was one big, happy family with everyone acquainted with one another. Sometimes there would be several people conversing on the line, as one after the other would join in the conversation. How well I remember chatting with Mary, to suddenly hear someone say, "That you, Mary?" and we would soon have a three-way conversation going.

Even before I met her in person, I knew I was going to like Mary, for her friendly personality, cheerful voice and jolly laughter fairly lit up the party line. "How very much like Mom," I concluded one day as I hung up the receiver after chattering away with Mary just as though she were my own mother. Mary was great therapy for our countryside. I remember her best as someone to call on in time of need. When my babies were not feeling well, Mary's instructions over the phone soon had mother and babies feeling better.

Mary's large, white, homey farmhouse was up a picturesque, winding country lane at the foot of Locust Hill mountain. Our farmhouse was several miles from Mary's home on the next mountain. She had more than enough to keep her busy on her own farm, but she always found time for others. If we did not have a sitter when we were going square dancing at the grange hall, Mary would call over the party line and say, "Bring the kids on over; we'll get along just fine!" And they did, with Mary fussing over them just like they were her very own grandchildren. When we arrived to pick up the youngsters after midnight, Mary would have one on each knee, visiting merrily away as they all rocked to and fro in a large, comfortable rocking chair in the parlor. Close by, our baby snoozed in an old-fashioned cradle that had been brought out for the occasion.

Mary was also known far and wide for her cooking, especially her cart-wheel sugar cookies. In all the years that I knew her, I never knew her to be out of those temptingly delicious cookies. Somehow, she always managed to have some in reserve for everyone who visited her farm, especially the children, who all seemed to have a special place in her heart. Seldom would Mary forget to ask the children, "Would you like to have some sugar cookies?" There was one time when she did forget to ask my children, and they finally asked her if she were going to ask them to have some sugar cookies, much to my embarrassment. Mary chuckled merrily as she hurried into the pantry, soon to reappear with a tray of cookies and a pitcher of bubbling milk.

As a bride and later as a young mother miles away from family and friends, my problems would often seem insurmountable, but then I would think of Mary, who was just a party line away. Talking things over with her on the line soon brightened up my little world. I was not lonely again, for I had found a friend. She and I remained friends for many years on Locust Hill, then continued to be fast friends even after my husband and I moved away. I'm convinced that the "Marys" of the world are few and far between; perhaps this is why they are so special!

Helen Oakley

Creamy Butter Fudge

Makes approximately 50 pieces

3 cups granulated sugar
½ cup cocoa
⅛ teaspoon salt
1 tablespoon unflavored gelatin
1 cup whipping cream
½ cup milk

¼ cup light corn syrup
½ cup butter
½ cup margarine
1½ teaspoons vanilla
1½ cups chopped walnuts *or* pecans

Combine all ingredients, except vanilla and nuts, in a heavy 4-quart saucepan; blend well. Bring to a rolling boil, stirring constantly. Continue to cook until mixture registers 234° (soft-ball stage) on a candy thermometer; gradually lower heat and stir gently. Remove from heat; pour into bowl. Cool 20 minutes; add vanilla and beat with mixer on low speed until creamy. Stir in nuts. Spread into a 9-inch square pan. Cool and cut into squares.

No-Cook Divinity

Makes about 45 pieces

1 7-ounce package fluffy white icing mix
⅓ cup light corn syrup
1 teaspoon vanilla
½ cup boiling water
1 pound confectioners' sugar
½ cup finely chopped nuts

Combine icing mix, corn syrup, vanilla, and water in a small mixing bowl. Use electric mixer and beat on high speed until stiff peaks form. Transfer beaten mixture to a larger bowl and, on low speed, beat in confectioners' sugar a little at a time. Fold in nuts. Drop by teaspoonfuls onto waxed paper and top with additional nuts or candied fruit. Allow to dry on top, then turn and dry bottoms. Dry 12 hours, turning pieces over once or twice. Store in an air-tight container.

Almond Brittle

Makes approximately 35 pieces

1 cup coarsely chopped almonds *or* peanuts
1 cup butter
1⅓ cups sugar
1 tablespoon light corn syrup
3 tablespoons water

Spread almonds in shallow pan; toast at 250-300° until lightly browned. Leave in oven at 200° until ready to use. Melt butter in heavy 2-quart saucepan; stir in sugar, corn syrup and water. Heat until candy thermometer registers 234° (soft-ball stage). Quickly stir in warm almonds. Continue to cook to 295° (hard-crack stage), stirring frequently. Pour onto buttered marble slab or cookie sheet and spread out as thinly as possible. Break into pieces when cool.

Note: **Do not** use a substitute for butter.

The Class Reunion

Remember the old one-room school-
house, dear friend,
Which was built to house grades one to
eight?
Remember the old recitation bench
On which boys carved initials and
names?
Remember the prayer and salute to the
flag
That each pupil had learned by heart?
Remember the ring of the old school-
house bell
As it echoed across the schoolyard?

Remember the change to the big school
  in town
With its halls and its multiple rooms?
Remember the rides on the bright
  yellow bus
Which ran from September till June?
Remember the junior and senior proms?
Remember new friendships we made?
Remember the tears that were silently
  shed
On that graduation day?

Remember the new halls of ivy some
  chose
In search of a higher degree?
Remember the ones who decided to sail
The great sea of matrimony?
Remember? Remember? is heard
  everywhere
As classmates assemble again
To rekindle old memories and friend-
  ships renew
At the happy-time class reunion.

Loise Pinkerton Fritz

Photo Overleaf
ST. NICOLAS, MINNESOTA
Grant Heilman Photography

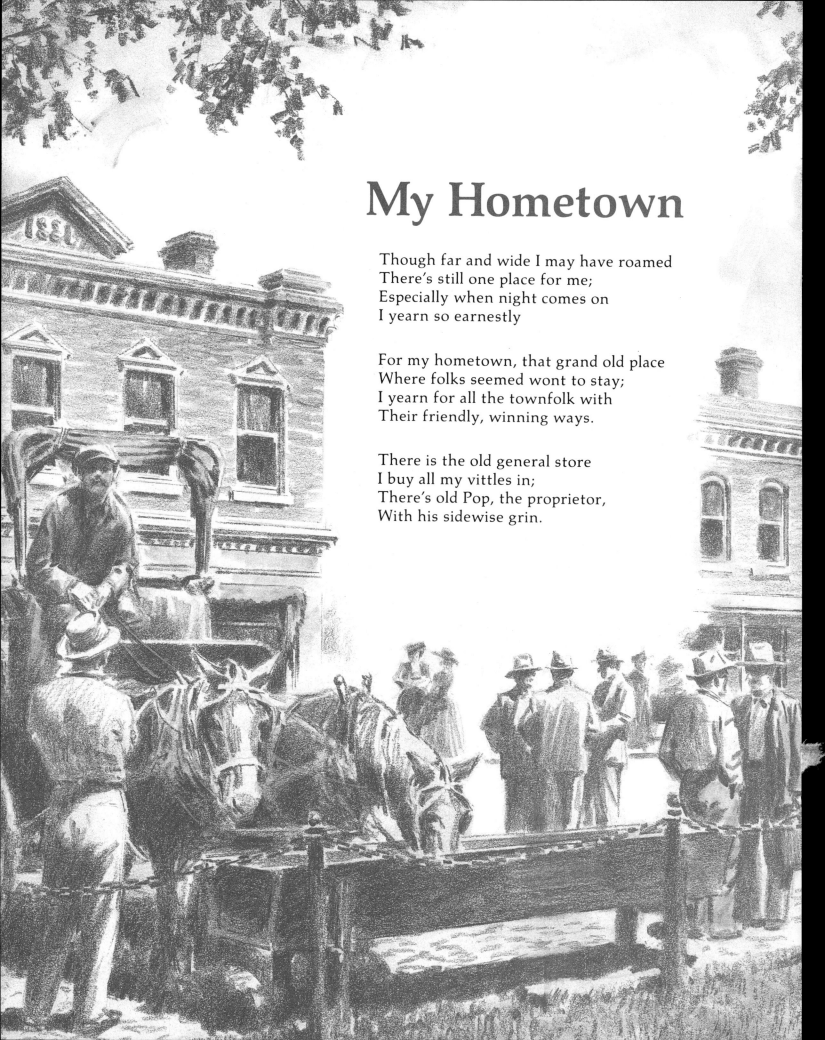

My Hometown

Though far and wide I may have roamed
There's still one place for me;
Especially when night comes on
I yearn so earnestly

For my hometown, that grand old place
Where folks seemed wont to stay;
I yearn for all the townfolk with
Their friendly, winning ways.

There is the old general store
I buy all my vittles in;
There's old Pop, the proprietor,
With his sidewise grin.

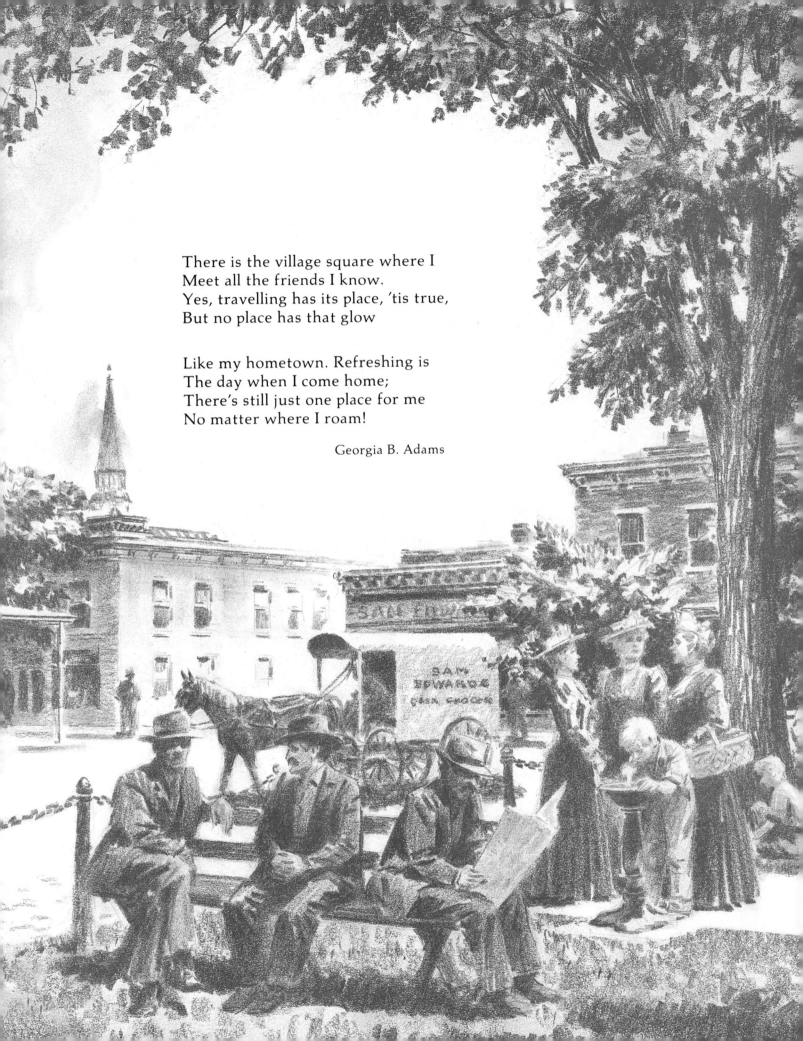

There is the village square where I
Meet all the friends I know.
Yes, travelling has its place, 'tis true,
But no place has that glow

Like my hometown. Refreshing is
The day when I come home;
There's still just one place for me
No matter where I roam!

Georgia B. Adams

Golden Friendship

Each golden friendship I have known
Is like a guiding star
That leads me through the yesteryears
Of places near and far.

The large and little cities and
The streets of long ago,
Where life was merely part of all
The winds that used to blow.

Each helping hand and loving smile
Is like a song of old,
Imbued with all the melody
I wish that I could hold.

And though the hours still to come
May be a million more,
I dream about the happiness
That filled my heart before.

I see the faces young and bright
That meant so much to me,
And their endearing friendship is
My fondest memory.

James J. Metcalfe

Photo Opposite
EDGARTOWN EVENING
Mary Jane Hayes

Our Friendship

Our friendship has grown
Through many long years,
Made sweeter by laughter,
Made stronger by tears.

Our friendship will mirror
In long years ahead
The wisdom of silence
With vain words unsaid.

Our friendship will echo
All down through the years
With words that bring laughter
And wipe away tears.

Our friendship is lasting
Because it reflects
A kind understanding
And mutual respect.

Josephine Millard

Souvenirs of Friendship

Our paths so long together twined
Must now go differently,
And you, my friend, will soon depart
To move away from me.

The souvenirs of friendship
That I keep within my heart
Will serve to join us still as friends
Though we may be apart.

These souvenirs are treasures rare—
A spritely gay hello,
A special look of fond respect
That only friends can know.

A cheerful smile, a heartfelt tear,
A spirit bright and gay,
A simple chat, a quiet walk,
A wave across the way.

These souvenirs will be with me
To strengthen and to cheer,
To let me know that we are friends,
Although we are not near.

Craig E. Sathoff

The Path to a
Friend's Home
Is Never Long.

ABCDEFGHIJKLM
NOPQRSTUVWXYZ

FRIENDSHIP

STL ♥♥ 1986

Universal Prayer

My friends are all a part of me—
Intangible and dear—
That make mosaics of my heart
And keep their presence near.

I owe so much to all of them,
Life scattered here and there;
I want to put my feelings down
And mail them everywhere.

I try to write one giant verse
Including every friend;
Alas! Each day brings more to say—
My musings find no end.

And so instead of verse I choose
A universal prayer:
"God bless them every one," I ask,
"And let them know I care."

June Masters Bacher

Editor's Note: The counted cross-stitch design opposite was designed especially for **ideals**®. If you would like a copy of the graph, please send a self-addressed, stamped envelope to Cross-Stitch Graph, c/o Ideals Editorial, P.O. Box 141000, Nashville, TN 37214-1000.

Welcome Signs

An empty chair, an open door,
A welcome mat in view;
These are the special welcome signs
That I extend to you.

A teapot on the kitchen stove,
Some cookies in the jar,
An attitude of friendly ease—
Come just the way you are.

A heart that longs for fellowship,
A heart that loves to share,
A heart that lives with homespun ways
Is waiting for you there.

So if you have the time, please come
To visit for a while.
There is a pleasure to be found
In simple homespun style.

Craig Sathoff

Friendship in a Cup

Come sit, my friend,
    And let us share
New warmth, with kindness
    Stirring there.
The work and toil
    Put aside,
Relax for now,
    With me confide.

Let's chat awhile
    And sip our brew,
You'll trust in me
    And I'll trust in you.
We'll whisper of
    Our special needs,
Then praise each other's
    Thoughts and deeds.

We'll laugh and sing,
    We'll make up rhymes,
And know that these
    Are special times.
This simple cup,
    So oft' ignored
Rekindles friendship,
    Faith restored.

Then, later, when life's
    Much to bear—
Come sit, my friend,
    And let us share...

C.L. Serra

A Friend's Visit

Today your note was in the mail
That said you'd come to stay
And visit us a day or two
When you passed our way.

What joy was deep within my heart
The welcome news to know,
That once again I'd talk with you
As in the years ago.

For friendship that is true and good
Does not dim with the years
But stays alive within the heart
Where it is ever dear.

Although I think of you each day
And always will, my friend,
No thoughts can equal half the joy
Of seeing you again.

Craig E. Sathoff

Photo Opposite
STAY IN TOUCH
Joanne Kash

Reward

When I was young I had a friend
Who listened with her heart;
We shared our joys, our griefs, our dreams,
And mapped our future chart.

And then she heard a distant drum—
I stayed with lonely tears;
And memories of youth grew dim,
Absorbed by miles and years.

But though the mind forgets the past,
The heart is never free;
The friend I loved so long ago
Has walked through life with me.

Helen Castle

Chance Meeting

I met an old friend today,
And I smiled through my tears;
I had so often thought of her,
But we'd not met for years.

Time had made many changes
In her life and in mine,
But despite the graying hair,
My old friend was looking fine.

I could not ask for a brighter day,
Could think of no joy to compare;
With that of meeting my old friend,
The world became gloriously fair.

Estelle D. Broadrick

Porch Sittin'

Used to be everybody had a porch, and everybody used it. Today, few people do more than dash in from the rain under the protection of a small stoop or pause to ring the doorbell.

Young people need to revive the lost art of "porch sittin'." Personally, I'm glad to see a bit of renewal of this old custom in the growing popularity of the old house plans with their large front porches. Sometimes in my travels about the countryside, I see people sitting comfortably out on a porch, letting time roll under their feet, passing time or waiting for that occasional "drop-in" visitor. When I see a scene like this, I can't help but wonder whatever happened to all the sitters... and the front porches that they sat upon.

As newer houses developed, the side porch became popular. Following closely behind came the modern porch stoop, while decks and patios took over the rear of the house. As communities became more thickly populated, people felt they needed more privacy. But back a generation or so ago, sitting on your porch was just a way of being neighborly.

When I was a child, we didn't have a very big porch, but I sat on it just the same. As a matter of fact, I did a lot of things on that porch. I discovered, all in due time, that porches were good for kissing on, crying on and "breaking up" on, too. Because we didn't have air-conditioning, we often entertained our company out on the porch or in the yard. Across the road at my grandmother's was a huge, old two-story house with a front porch that covered its entire width. That was where I spent some of my most memorable afternoons, sitting in a chair with my bare feet propped up against a porch column while listening to my aunts, keeping an eye on the wasps' nest just above my head, and waiting for the ice cream to harden.

Porches were a means of escape for me, but somehow Mama always knew where to find me. In the late afternoons after all my chores were done, I just liked to sit out there and gaze out at the stars or listen to the sounds of a gentle country night. I was never scared out there on the porch. Some nights I even got out of bed and went out there to think when my mind was jumbled up with decisions and the disturbing pain of youth.

Memories of summer porches in my childhood are endless: my mama cutting corn off the cob, transferring tubs of water to the old wringer washing machine; my brothers pushing their toy trucks along the well-kept and painted board floor or cutting a watermelon for an afternoon snack.

We could learn a lot from our ancestors, who made a regular habit of sitting out on the porch. Though hard-working people, they apparently also knew the value of relaxation. They knew that balance was the key to good living. After all, look at what they left behind for us as a gentle reminder—the rocking chair.

The rocking chair was a virtual haven and necessity for "porch sittin'." When you take a rocking chair out of your house and put it on the porch, you immediately intensify the pleasure of rocking by adding summer fragrances and the sounds of nature. Even peeling onions or shelling beans becomes more enjoyable when you add a rocking chair to the porch. And if you're lucky enough to own a swing, you're in for a glorious treat indeed. There's nothing in the whole world quite like grasping the chains of a swing and trying to touch the sky with your toes... or in this case, the porch ceiling. Add a broad-brimmed straw hat for fanning, and your "porch sittin'" becomes complete.

Even if you've only got a small porch, find the space for a chair or two, maybe even a swing. Begin by sitting out there just by yourself, only you and the sounds of the late afternoon and the smells of the yard that surrounds you. Take the time out there on your porch to look, listen, observe, smell and sense the special things in life. Take it all in. Be aware of the gentle reminders from the past that time is fleeting. Try hard. Try more than once. You just might succeed in bringing back the tranquil way of life that reigned for more than a century, back before we all became lost in making a living and getting ahead.

"Porch sittin'" is a lesson in life passed along from our ancestors. It seems they knew more than we thought they did.

Gail L. Roberson

Painting Opposite, LEMONADE TIME, John Walters

Because You Are
My Friend

I'm glad we met, dear friend,
On that day so long ago.
"By chance," we said and yet I think
That God had willed it so.

Your friendly way has brought me cheer,
The thoughtful things you do;
It means so much to have a friend
Who's always warm and true.

You are the one to whom I turn
When trouble comes my way;
You somehow help my heart to see
There'll come a brighter day.

My world's a brighter place
And I'd like for you to know—
It's because you are my friend
That helps to make it so.

Kay Hoffman

Maturity and Friends

True friends are a treasure
We don't fully realize.
For when we are young
We aren't so very wise.

But as we grow older
We come to understand
That real, true friendship
Offers a trusting hand.

Don't get busy and neglect friends,
Get in touch and don't delay.
Time goes by so quickly
You may not have another day.

So if you want to have friends,
Just keep this thought in mind:
Let them know that you love them—
True friends are hard to find.

Anna Bell Henry Steen

Seashore Song

The sun-drenched hours
   Are sweet and long
Where summer sings
   Her siren song,
And time stands still
   While tots explore
Sweet mysteries
   Of sea and shore;
No school bells ring
   To spoil the day
Of happy children
   Hard at play.

Where wavelets kiss
   Bright seaside sands,
Small Sandra laughs
   And claps her hands
And seems to never,
   Never tire
Of splashing mists
   Of silver fire;
A water nymph
   With golden hair,
She makes a lovely
   picture there.

Beneath her mother's
   Watchful eye,
She chases waves
   That scurry by
And searches waters
   Crystal clear
To see where
   Sunbeams disappear.
Adventure waits
   Where ripples swirl
Around a gleeful
   Little girl.

Brian F. King

Remembered Friends

Remembered friends, like trading ships
That beach on memory's shore,
Can bring back thoughts of yesterday
And then go back for more.

Remembered friends, like harnessed sun
Against a stormy day,
Can find a window of the mind
And shine the gloom away.

Remembered friends, like a treasured rose
That climbs around the door,
Though petals fall, the heart remains
To bloom forevermore.

June Masters Bacher

Old Times, Old Friends

Old times, old friends, how dear are these
To treasure now in memories.
Whatever marked each passing day
Has left its imprint on life's way.

The joyous years that swiftly passed,
In blessed remembrance still will last.
The ones we loved, no longer here,
In memory's chambers still are near.

How true that precious joys live yet,
That there are things we can't forget.
Old times, old friends, how dear are these
To treasure now in memories.

Agnes Davenport Bond

A Garden

As I wander among the flowers, I fondly touch each one,
And see the bees and hummingbirds sip honey in the sun.
A mockingbird is singing in the highest tree,
And the sky is cobalt blue as far as I can see.

A spider web is shimmering with the morning dew,
And violets among the ferns are hiding safe from view.
Spicy pinks beside the path, tiger lillies tall
Nod to the honeysuckle climbing o'er the wall.

The roses are my favorites, the sweet peas are divine.
Hollyhocks are tall as giants, carnations are sublime.
A lovely fragrance fills the air from many different flowers;
This is such a lovely place to spend one's idle hours.

Doris Cox

Summer Rain

What could be lovelier than to hear
the summer rain
cutting across the heat, as scythes
cut across grain?
falling upon the steaming roof
with sweet uproar,
tapping and rapping wildly
at the door?

No, do not lift the latch,
but through the pane
we'll watch the circus pageant
of the rain,
and see the tiger lightning,
striped and dread,
and hear the thunder shake the sky
with elephant tread.

Elizabeth Coatsworth

Rain

It's such a joy to stroll a lane
After a soft, cool summer rain,
And smell the fragrance lingering fair
Of honeysuckle on the air.
I like to feel upon my face
The kiss of raindrops as they race
To freshen up the earth again
With cool, refreshing summer rain.

As children, one joy to attain
Was walking barefoot in the rain,
And feel the gentle, soft caress
Of raindrops—oh, what happiness!
Though childhood days have long since passed
Their pleasant memories ever last
To bring to us the joy again
Of walking barefoot in the rain.

Carice Williams

Have You Looked at the Sky Today?

Today the sky is azure blue,
But you have many things to do.
You're thankful just to make it through—
    Have you looked at the sky today?

The fleecy clouds are piled on high,
Like lofty galleons sailing by;
No time is there to lift the eye—
    Have *you* looked at the sky today?

The sun goes down, a flaming red;
The after-glow is widely spread.
You're spent from earning daily bread—
    Have you *looked* at the sky today?

The stars illume the dark, cool night;
The waxing moon is clear and bright.
But you can only feel uptight—
    Have you looked *at* the sky today?

There's beauty, vision, courage, hope.
There's grace and strength to help you cope;
You need not always vainly grope—
    Have you looked at the *sky* today?

We need this skyward look each day,
To guide us in life's upward way;
Restore us when we go astray—
    Have you looked at the sky *today*?

J. Harold Gwynne

Nancy Ward: Friend of the Pioneers

For the pioneers who were struggling to establish settlements in the wilderness of the Cumberland Mountains, the protection of sparsely-located forts was often not enough. They needed supporters and friends among the tribes of Indians who were growing increasingly restless over broken treaties and the constant invasions of their lands. Such a friend was found in Nancy (*Nanye-hi*) Ward, last Beloved Woman of the Cherokee nation.

Nanye-hi ("spirit people") was born in 1738 to Tame Doe, who was the sister of a Cherokee chief. In the early 1750's, Tame Doe arranged for *Nanye-hi* to marry Kingfisher, a Cherokee warrior who lived near Chote, the Cherokee capitol, in eastern Tennessee. In 1755, *Nanye-hi* followed her husband into a battle with the Creeks. When Kingfisher was

Nancy (*Nanye-hi*) Ward, last Cherokee Beloved Woman, is pictured in this painting by Chattanooga artist Ben Hampton (photograph courtesy of the Tennessee State Library and Archives, Nashville).

killed, *Nanye-hi* picked up his rifle and continued fighting. Her bravery inspired the other members of her tribe, and she led them on to a victory over the Creeks. Word of her heroic action spread among the Cherokees, and prompted the Council of Chiefs to choose her as *Aqi-qa-u-e*, Beloved Woman.

The Beloved Woman was the most honored woman in the Cherokee's strongly matriarchal society. She was head of the Women's Council and was a member of the powerful Council of Chiefs. The Beloved Woman also helped prepare warriors for battle and was involved in the planning sessions for battles.

Although *Nanye-hi* was not yet twenty years old when she was chosen as Beloved Woman, she handled her duties with resourcefulness and wisdom. The last half of the eighteenth century was a time of crisis and turmoil in the South. France and England were in constant conflict over territorial claims, and the frontier settlers often feuded with the English—a sign of the Revolution to come. All three sides tried to involve the Cherokees in the land squabbles, complicating the internal strife the Cherokees were having over land sales and treaty negotiations.

In 1757, *Nanye-hi* married Bryant Ward, a white trader from South Carolina. From this marriage, she took the name of Nancy Ward, and became familiar with some of the white settlers' views and customs. She saw a great need for peace, and often used her influence in the Council of Chiefs to counsel tolerance toward the growing number of white settlers as well as promoting peace between the warring factions of her own tribe. When talk failed, Nancy took actions which proved her growing friendship for the pioneers.

In 1776, Nancy warned settlers of a plan to attack the Watauga fort in eastern Tennessee. Her warning gave the station time to fortify, and the pioneers were able to withstand a two-week siege by the Cherokees. Nancy even worked to save the one white settler which the Cherokees captured. Lydia Bean was caught outside the fort and taken to a nearby village for execution by fire. Nancy Ward arrived and reportedly declared, "No woman shall be burned at the stake while I am Beloved Woman." Mrs. Bean repaid Nancy by teaching her more of the white settlers' customs, including how to make cheese and butter from cow's milk.

Four years later, Nancy again warned the Wataugan settlers of an impending attack. This time the Cherokees were defeated and a peace council was held in July, 1781. In spite of her warnings, Nancy was seldom thought of as a traitor by the Cherokees. Even the most militant factions of the tribe recognized and respected her push for peace. As a result, Nancy was the first Indian woman to actively engage in the treaty negotiations and was the featured speaker at the council of July, 1781. She spoke to the gathering with dramatic eloquence: "Our cry is for peace . . . This peace must last forever. Let your women's sons be ours; our sons be yours. Let your women hear our words."

Following that Treaty of Long Island, the majority of Cherokees lived in peace with the white settlers. There were still a few warring chiefs who refused to honor the treaty, and in 1783, Nancy once again used her influence as Beloved Woman to save two white settlers. The men had gone among the Cherokees carrying hidden weapons, which the Cherokees considered an act of aggression. They would have killed the men had Nancy not intervened.

Nancy Ward continued to serve as Beloved Woman until her death in about 1820. For almost fifty years she had been an exceptional leader of the Cherokee nation, continually pushing for friendship and peace with the pioneers. She spoke at many treaty councils, including the 1785 Treaty of Hopewell (South Carolina) during which she presented the treaty commissioners with a chain of beads, symbolic of a chain of friendship. "We hope the chain of friendship will never more be broken." It was a hope for which Nancy Ward stood throughout her career as Beloved Woman of the Cherokee nation and loyal friend of the pioneers.

Ilene J. Cornwell

Song of the Grandmother

I am Cherokee.
My people believe in the Spirit that unites all
  things.
I am woman. I am life force. My word has great
  value.
The man reveres me as he reveres Mother Earth
  and his own spirit.

The Beloved Woman is one of our principal
  chiefs.
Through her the Spirit often speaks to the people.
In the Great Council at the capital she is a
  powerful voice.
Concerning the fate of hostages, her word is
  absolute.

Women share in all of life. We lead sacred
  dances.
In the Council we debate freely with men until an
  agreement is reached.
When the nation considers war, we have a say,
For we bear the warriors. Sometimes we go into
  battle.
We also plant and harvest.

I carry my own name and the name of my clan.
If I accept a mate, he and our children take the
  name of my clan. If there is deep trouble
  between us,
I am as free to tell him to go as he is to leave.
Our children and our dwelling stay with me.
So long as I am treated with dignity, I am
  steadfast.

I love and work and sing.
I listen to the Spirit.
In all things I speak my mind.
I walk without fear.
I am Cherokee.

Marilou Awiakta

Friendship

Friendship is a precious word,
We treasure it with care;
Life without our special friends
Would be forlorn and bare.

Friends, like garden flowers, grow
From seed and bud and bloom
Within the garden of the heart
In a chosen corner room.

Within our daily thoughts they live
Surrounded by our love.
Friends, like garden flowers,
Are gifts from heaven above.

Eleanor Fiock

Mrs. Paul E. King

Mrs. King was born in Gratz, Pennsylvania, and grew up on her family's farm in Lykens Valley, where she began to write poems and stories by the age of nine. In her words: "My parents' lovely old farm...was situated against a mountain, with purling streams issuing through my father's fertile fields. Nature surrounded me! I had to express my feelings! I still do. There is so much beauty everywhere: one need but to look to see it."

Mrs. King's first writings were for friends and relatives, but her audience soon expanded. She is the author of *The Children's Hour*, a book of stories for children, and is a regular contributor to *The Missionary Revivalist*. She also writes and edits *The Sunday School Beacon* for her general church. A minister's wife for 36 years, Mrs. King enjoys working with church music programs as well as her gardening, reading and writing. *Ideals* has published many of her fine poems, and we are now proud to feature her as Best-Loved Poet.

Making Ice Cream

What fun and oh, the merriment!
How bright our eyes did gleam,
Turning the handle round and round,
Making rich ice cream.

The hand-turned bucket filled with ice,
And rock salt layered between,
Squeaked and groaned as the handle went round,
Making delicious ice cream.

Each had his turn at cranking the handle.
We worked till our arms were sore,
And kept the old handle churning and turning,
Till it just wouldn't turn anymore.

Then, "Come and get it!" our father would shout,
And his eyes held a wonderful gleam.
Ours was a closely-knit family for sure,
When making homemade ice cream.

When Mother Read To Me

At evening when the fires were lit,
When lights were burning bright,
I snuggled up in Mother's lap,
A carefree little sprite.
My head I pillowed on her breast,
From cares my mind was free;
I found the moments so divine
When Mother read to me.

She read me tales of far-off lands,
Of pretty fairies, gay,
And of the goblins that come round
On every Halloween Day.
I was carried on a ship to Spain
Or to a mountain high
Where I would touch the fleecy clouds
That drifted so idly by.

I sailed the wild, tempestuous sea,
And scaled Mount Shasta's height;
I even hunted wild elephants
In Africa at night.
Oh! I'd go clear around the world
From Mother's lap . . . you see,
I was a brave adventurer
When Mother read to me.

Canning Time

It's canning time and the house is a-flutter.
There're jars everywhere and the kitchen's a-clutter.
Our meals are quite lean and quickly prepared,
For there's work to be done and all have a share.

The relish and chow-chow, so fragrant and hot,
Bubble over so gently in big separate pots.
While catsup and grape butter (really a treat)
All simmer nearby so spicy and sweet.

There're jars of pickles and jars of corn
All freshly canned since early morn;
And jars of beets and petite peas
All packed in nicely and sure to please.

Fall Is Everywhere

The frost is in the meadow,
And the pumpkins, big and round,
Are glowing among the fodder shocks
And brightening up the ground.

The purple grapes and bittersweet
Hang heavy on the vine,
While apples, pears and hickory nuts
Bespeak of harvest time.

There's a haze hung o'er the valley,
Pungent leaf smoke fills the air,
Squirrels gather nuts industriously,
And fall is everywhere.

The creek bed wears a cover
Of thin ice in early dawn;
The crimson rose is faded blue
And her blossom's almost gone.

The trees are decked in colors bright,
Each bush a gay, bright cloak does wear,
The earth smells sweetly fragrant
And fall is everywhere.

A Boy's Point of View

There's a tantalizin' odor
Comin' up the windin' stair;
An' it sets my mouth to waterin',
Smells like perfume in the air.

Not just an ordinary perfume
Like the lassies keep around,
But this tantalizin' odor
Smells like turkey roastin' brown.

Or a kind of spicy goodness
(Can't forget it if I try)
Draws me like a great strong magnet
To my mother's pumpkin pie.

An' this temptin' kind of odor
Makes me want to shout "Hooray!"
There's no need for me to tell you
That today's Thanksgiving Day!

Wellspring

Do you go by the spring
Let the dipper sink slow—
Hurry troubles the water, you know,
And makes you sit on your heels in the fern
Waitin' for the water to settle and turn
Not near so clear as it was.
So . . . let the dipper sink slow.

Do you feel a song stir
Be still and lay low—
Gentle it like a fawn from the wood
With a silent croon that's understood.
Don't nothin' start quicker'n a fawn
Lessen maybe it's a song.
So . . . be still and lay low.
Let the dipper sink slow.

Do you find a new friend
On his hill, leave him be—
So he can welcome himself as he will
Bidin' or not with you on your hill.
Come a day though lyin' a valley apart
You'll have souls a-growin' up heart to heart.
So . . . leave a friend be.

Marilou Awiakta

From **Abiding Appalachia: Where Mountain and Atom Meet** by Marilou
Awiakta. St. Luke's Press, Memphis, 1978.

Photo Opposite
LOWER PROXY FALLS
Jeff Gnass

Late Summer

The days lie quiet like a child asleep,
And winds no longer rustle full-grown leaves.
The farmer must not wait while summer grieves,
For ripening grain is ready now to reap.
While shadows lengthen and the sun sets deep
Within the west, the hurrying farmer weaves
And ties a band around small perfect sheaves
Of gold. For him illusive summers creep...

Then pass too soon! He knows the summer sun
Has sealed her secret in the golden grain;
She worked as though her task had just begun;
For soon she knew the early autumn rain
Would come and harvesting must then be done.
Late summer always sings a glad refrain!

May Smith White

The Sound of Autumn

I heard the sound of autumn
As I trod the woods today,
And it was then I knew full well
That summer could not stay.
Summer, with its carefree days,
Its fields of scented clover,
Would soon be just a memory
While autumn would take over.

I heard the call of autumn,
It sounded loud and clear;
And though the summer sun still shone,
Jack Frost would soon be here.
The lovely, lovely summertime
Would soon be on its way,
For I heard the sound of autumn
In the calling of the jay.

Loise Pinkerton Fritz

Jack Frost Is Knocking on ideals® Door!

And with the first frost comes the glory of Autumn ideals®. Share with us those crisp, color-filled days of early fall when the fields are ready for the harvest, the kids are ready for school and the ghosts are ready for Halloween. You can also share the glorious colors of fall with a friend by giving a subscription, starting with our next issue, Autumn ideals® .

One of our friends, Mrs. Leroy Anderson of Crestwood, Illinois, recently shared with us her thoughts about ideals®.

"Hi, from a new and excited, first-time subscriber! Wow! I was impressed with the Christmas edition, and was going to give you a trial on the next one—just to see! It's the best gift I ever lavished on myself.

"Your SWEETHEART edition, as well as the CHRISTMAS one, gave me a sense of awesomeness. I read every word with such appreciation for the talents submitted. It's the most beautiful and rewarding magazine one could ever experience in a lifetime. I will cherish every one of them.

"Now I'm saving my money to start sharing my joy with my loved ones as presents. Thank you from the bottom of my heart for ideals®."

Thank you, Mrs. Anderson! We hope all our friends feel the same way and will let us know.

ACKNOWLEDGEMENTS

MY HOMETOWN by Georgia B. Adams, used by permission of her mother, Anna M. Adams; OLD TIMES, OLD FRIENDS by Agnes Davenport Bond, used by permission of her granddaughter, Mrs. Robert Childs; SUMMER RAIN, reprinted with permission of Macmillan Publishing Company from *POEMS* by Elizabeth Coatsworth, copyright 1940 by Macmillan Publishing Company, renewed 1968 by Elizabeth Coatsworth Beston; A GARDEN by Doris Cox, used by permission of her daughter, Kathryn L. Smith; GETTING HOME by Edgar A. Guest, used by permission of his daughter, Janet Guest Sobell; A FRIEND by Edith M. Helstern, used by permission of her friend, Virginia J. Cooper; GOLDEN FRIENDSHIP by James J. Metcalfe, used by permission of his son, James Metcalfe, Jr. Our sincere thanks to the following whose addresses we were unable to locate: Helen Castle for REWARD; Louise Darcy for TO A CAT ON HER 14th BIRTHDAY; the estate of Eleanor Fiock for FRIENDSHIP; Lonna Hall for THE HIDING PLACE; the estate of Betty Hunter for SONNETS; the estate of Brian F. King for SEASHORE SONG; Josephine Millard for OUR FRIENDSHIP; May Smith White for LATE SUMMER.